KU-542-408

★ ★ ★ ★ ★ ★ ★ ★ ★ ★ ★ ★

YOU MAY BE

60

But You've Still

GOT IT

★ ★ ★ ★ ★ ★ ★ ★ ★ ★ ★ ★

summersdale

YOU MAY BE 60 BUT YOU'VE STILL GOT IT

Summersdale Publishers Ltd
46 West Street
Chichester
West Sussex
PO19 1RP
UK

www.summersdale.com

Printed and bound in China

ISBN: 978-1-84953-349-2

Substantial discounts on bulk quantities of Summersdale books are available to corporations, professional associations and other organisations. For details contact Nicky Douglas by telephone: +44 (0) 1243 756902, fax: +44 (0) 1243 786300 or email: nicky@summersdale.com.

23.03.14.

To Valerie

Love from

From Anne-Marie x

* * * * * * * * * * * *

GROW OLD ALONG WITH ME! WITH ME! THE BEST IS YET TO BE...

ROBERT BROWNING

* * * * * * * * * * * *

* * * * * * * * * * * *

Now *you're 60,* it's the
perfect time to set aside
your reservations and
become the person you
truly *want to be.*

* * * * * * * * * * * *

* * * * * * * * * * *

If you don't have one already, get a *computer* and get connected to the *Internet!* There's a whole world of information to enjoy.

* * * * * * * * * * *

★ ★ ★ ★ ★ ★ ★ ★ ★ ★ ★ ★

On a *warm night,* go for an evening *picnic* with your partner or a friend.

★ ★ ★ ★ ★ ★ ★ ★ ★ ★ ★ ★

* * * * * * * * * * * *

Volunteer your time to
an animal shelter or any
other *charity* which
means a lot to you.

* * * * * * * * * * * *

IT'S BETTER TO TRAVEL HOPEFULLY THAN TO ARRIVE.

* * * * * * * * * * *

If you have friends or
family that *live abroad*
and you've been meaning
to *visit,* arrange it now —
there's no time like
the present!

* * * * * * * * * * *

* * * * * * * * * * *

Secure a *hammock* between two trees in your garden and relax in the sunshine. If you don't have trees, splash out on a luxurious *lawn chair*.

* * * * * * * * * * *

* * * * * * * * * * *

If you're able to,
donate blood and
help *save lives.*

* * * * * * * * * * *

LIFE IS WHAT YOU MAKE IT.

★ ★ ★ ★ ★ ★ ★ ★ ★ ★ ★ ★

Read a *classic novel* that you've never got round to; perhaps something by *Dickens, Tolstoy* or the *Brontë* sisters.

★ ★ ★ ★ ★ ★ ★ ★ ★ ★ ★ ★

★ ★ ★ ★ ★ ★ ★ ★ ★ ★ ★ ★

Take the time to get to know
your *neighbours* – invite
them round for a cup of tea
or bake them a *cake.*

★ ★ ★ ★ ★ ★ ★ ★ ★ ★ ★ ★

★ ★ ★ ★ ★ ★ ★ ★ ★ ★ ★ ★ ★

Wear an *outfit* that
nobody would *ever expect*
to see you in.

★ ★ ★ ★ ★ ★ ★ ★ ★ ★ ★ ★ ★

★ ★ ★ ★ ★ ★ ★ ★ ★ ★ ★ ★

Increase your *geographical knowledge* by learning all the counties in your country – perhaps even *pay a visit* to one you've never heard of.

★ ★ ★ ★ ★ ★ ★ ★ ★ ★ ★ ★

TO REMAIN
YOUNG WHILE
GROWING OLD
IS THE HIGHEST
BLESSING.

✦ ✦ ✦ ✦ ✦ ✦ ✦ ✦ ✦ ✦ ✦ ✦

Put *potted plants* around
your home. They will make
the atmosphere much more
pleasant and nurturing them
will give you a sense of
achievement.

✦ ✦ ✦ ✦ ✦ ✦ ✦ ✦ ✦ ✦ ✦ ✦

* * * * * * * * * * * *

Volunteer to look after a
friend or family member's
young *children,* and take
them to a local pond to
feed the ducks.

* * * * * * * * * * * *

* * * * * * * * * * * *

Explore your
family's history and
see how far into the past
you can *trace* it back to.

* * * * * * * * * * * *

* * * * * * * * * * * *

If life gives you lemons,
make *lemonade*... literally!
You just need sugar, water,
and freshly squeezed
lemon juice.

* * * * * * * * * * * *

★ ★ ★ ★ ★ ★ ★ ★ ★ ★ ★ ★

AGE IS THE RIPENING, THE SWELLING, OF THE FRESH LIFE WITHIN, THAT WITHERS AND BURSTS THE HUSK.

GEORGE MACDONALD

★ ★ ★ ★ ★ ★ ★ ★ ★ ★ ★ ★

★ ★ ★ ★ ★ ★ ★ ★ ★ ★ ★

Go green and try using a bike to get around town. It's more relaxing than a car or bus and is good, *gentle exercise.*

★ ★ ★ ★ ★ ★ ★ ★ ★ ★ ★

* * * * * * * * * * *

Think about all the
blessings you have
in *your life.*

* * * * * * * * * * *

★ ★ ★ ★ ★ ★ ★ ★ ★ ★ ★ ★

Offer to spend your day
helping out a friend or
family member you know
is very *busy*.

★ ★ ★ ★ ★ ★ ★ ★ ★ ★ ★ ★

* * * * * * * * * * * *

Have your *caricature*
drawn by an artist, put it up
in your home and use it as a
reminder to not take life
too seriously.

* * * * * * * * * * * *

A ROLLING STONE GATHERS NO MOSS.

* * * * * * * * * * * *

Go to a *car boot sale* or
antiques fair and buy the
most *unusual* thing
you can find.

* * * * * * * * * * * *

* * * * * * * * * * * *

If you feel there's a
bit of a *thespian* in
you, why not join a local
amateur dramatics
society? If there isn't one,
start one.

* * * * * * * * * * * *

★ ★ ★ ★ ★ ★ ★ ★ ★ ★ ★ ★

Have a *fondue party.*
You can choose cheese
or chocolate or, if you're
feeling decadent, *both!*
(Separately, of course.)

★ ★ ★ ★ ★ ★ ★ ★ ★ ★ ★ ★

★ ★ ★ ★ ★ ★ ★ ★ ★ ★ ★ ★ ★

Build a magnificent
sandcastle on the beach.
Be sure to take pictures of it
before the *tide comes in.*

★ ★ ★ ★ ★ ★ ★ ★ ★ ★ ★ ★ ★

★ ★ ★ ★ ★ ★ ★ ★ ★

FOOTPRINTS
ON THE SANDS OF TIME ARE NOT MADE BY SITTING DOWN.

★ ★ ★ ★ ★ ★ ★ ★ ★

* * * * * * * * * * * *

Take a *boat* out on a
lake, river or canal and
enjoy *floating* along
in the fresh air.

* * * * * * * * * * * *

✶ ✶ ✶ ✶ ✶ ✶ ✶ ✶ ✶ ✶ ✶ ✶

Shake things up with a
new haircut – it will help
kick-start your *confidence*
and motivate you.

✶ ✶ ✶ ✶ ✶ ✶ ✶ ✶ ✶ ✶ ✶ ✶

* * * * * * * * * * * * *

Read a favourite *poem* or
passage, or contemplate
a favourite *piece of art.*
Pause to reflect on what it
means to you and how it
makes you feel.

* * * * * * * * * * * * *

* * * * * * * * * * * *

Go out for lunch and make
your *tip* for whoever serves
you that *little bit bigger*
than it would normally be.

* * * * * * * * * * * *

A THING OF BEAUTY IS A JOY FOREVER.

* * * * * * * * * * * *

Visit your local observatory
and give *stargazing* a
try, so you can enjoy the
wonders of the *universe.*

* * * * * * * * * * * *

* * * * * * * * * * * * *

Try to cook the most
vibrant and colourful
meal you can — as well as
looking tasty, different-
coloured foods will provide
you with a wider variety
of *nutrients.*

* * * * * * * * * * * * *

★ ★ ★ ★ ★ ★ ★ ★ ★ ★ ★ ★

Learn a few simple,
helpful phrases in several
foreign languages.
They may come in useful!

★ ★ ★ ★ ★ ★ ★ ★ ★ ★ ★ ★

YOU ARE NEVER TOO OLD TO LEARN.

★ ★ ★ ★ ★ ★ ★ ★ ★ ★ ★ ★ ★

Visit your local *library*
and take out all the books
that *catch your eye.*

★ ★ ★ ★ ★ ★ ★ ★ ★ ★ ★ ★ ★

* * * * * * * * * * * *

Go to that *restaurant*
that has been recommended
to you by friends or family,
but you never thought
was really 'your cup
of tea'. You may be
pleasantly surprised!

* * * * * * * * * * * *

* * * * * * * * * * * * *

At Christmas, Halloween
and other appropriate
times, *decorate* your
front garden or front door
extravagantly to
match the season.

* * * * * * * * * * * * *

* * * * * * * * * * * *

Take a *walk*, barefoot,
and *feel nature*
under your feet.

* * * * * * * * * * * *

MAKE HAY WHILE THE SUN SHINES.

★ ★ ★ ★ ★ ★ ★ ★ ★ ★ ★ ★

Go to a *music festival*
and show those young 'uns
how to have a *good time*.

★ ★ ★ ★ ★ ★ ★ ★ ★ ★ ★ ★

★ ★ ★ ★ ★ ★ ★ ★ ★ ★ ★ ★

Visit the *brewery,*
vineyard or distillery of your
favourite tipple.

★ ★ ★ ★ ★ ★ ★ ★ ★ ★ ★ ★

* * * * * * * * * * * *

If you have a number
of separate groups of
friends, *introduce* them
all. You never know what
new friendships
could begin.

* * * * * * * * * * * *

* * * * * * * * * * * *

I LOOK FORWARD
TO GROWING OLD
AND WISE AND
AUDACIOUS.

GLENDA JACKSON

* * * * * * * * * * * *

★ ★ ★ ★ ★ ★ ★ ★ ★ ★ ★ ★

Just because *you're 60,*
doesn't mean you have
to act your age! Play a
practical joke on a
friend (preferably one you
know won't take it the
wrong way).

★ ★ ★ ★ ★ ★ ★ ★ ★ ★ ★ ★

★ ★ ★ ★ ★ ★ ★ ★ ★ ★ ★ ★ ★

Read a book purely
on the recommendation
of a friend whose taste
you respect, but do not
necessarily always
agree with.

★ ★ ★ ★ ★ ★ ★ ★ ★ ★ ★ ★ ★

* * * * * * * * * * *

Go to the *zoo* with a friend
and *impersonate*
the animals.

* * * * * * * * * * *

* * * * * * * * * * * *

Get off the *bus* a stop early
to get more exercise and
enjoy the *fresh air*.

* * * * * * * * * * * *

SEIZE THE DAY!

* * * * * * * * * * * *

Try to find your way
through a *hedge maze*
at a *stately home* or
formal garden.

* * * * * * * * * * * *

* * * * * * * * * * * * *

When you next have reason to *celebrate,* treat yourself and a loved one to a meal and the *most expensive* wine on the menu at your favourite restaurant.

* * * * * * * * * * * * *

* * * * * * * * * * * * *

Take in some *culture*
with a night at the theatre
or opera, dressed in your
finest get-up.

* * * * * * * * * * * * *

★ ★ ★ ★ ★ ★ ★ ★ ★ ★ ★ ★

Think about what you have managed to *achieve* in your life so far, and set yourself a few goals that you want to achieve in the *coming decade.*

★ ★ ★ ★ ★ ★ ★ ★ ★ ★ ★ ★

★ ★ ★ ★ ★ ★ ★ ★ ★ ★ ★ ★

JUDGE EACH DAY NOT BY THE HARVEST YOU REAP BUT BY THE SEEDS YOU SOW.

ROBERT LOUIS STEVENSON

★ ★ ★ ★ ★ ★ ★ ★ ★ ★ ★ ★

Make *scones* for a posh afternoon tea:

★ Mix a pinch of salt with 225 g of flour, then rub in 55 g of butter.

★ Stir in 25 g of caster sugar and 150 ml of milk.

★ Knead the dough lightly and roll to 2 cm thick.

★ Cut out rounds and bake for about 15 minutes, until risen and golden.

★ ★ ★ ★ ★ ★ ★ ★ ★ ★ ★ ★

* * * * * * * * * * * *

If a loved one expresses an interest in a *hobby* of yours, take them under your wing and *teach them* about it.

* * * * * * * * * * * *

* * * * * * * * * * * *

Spend some time watching
the *wildlife* in your garden
or at your *local park*.

* * * * * * * * * * * *

★ ★ ★ ★ ★ ★ ★ ★ ★ ★ ★ ★

Write songs or poems about things you enjoy or admire and share the ones you're particularly *proud of* with others.

★ ★ ★ ★ ★ ★ ★ ★ ★ ★ ★ ★

★ ★ ★ ★ ★ ★ ★

OPPORTUNITY NEVER KNOCKS TWICE AT ANY MAN'S DOOR.

★ ★ ★ ★ ★ ★ ★

* * * * * * * * * * * *

If there's one *bad habit*
you know you have, try to
avoid doing it for a month.
After that, you may realise
you've stopped doing
it *altogether!*

* * * * * * * * * * * *

* * * * * * * * * * *

Give your *garden* a
unique charm by using
unusual planters like old
cups, tyres or suitcases – or,
if you have space, an old
rowing boat!

* * * * * * * * * * *

* * * * * * * * * * *

Go *food shopping* and
buy none of the essentials,
just what you fancy eating
that day. Chocolate, cheese,
champagne, or anything
indulgent.

* * * * * * * * * * *

★ ★ ★ ★ ★ ★ ★ ★ ★ ★ ★ ★

Organise a
scavenger hunt
around your house and
garden the next time
friends or family with
children visit.

★ ★ ★ ★ ★ ★ ★ ★ ★ ★ ★ ★

* * * * * * * * * * * *

THE TRICK
IS GROWING
UP WITHOUT
GROWING OLD.

CASEY STENGEL

* * * * * * * * * * * *

* * * * * * * * * * * *

Try your hand at
horse riding and go
out on a trail ride. It's the
perfect combination of
relaxing, learning new skills
and *adventure!*

* * * * * * * * * * * *

* * * * * * * * * * * *

Meet up with a friend
whilst they are on their lunch
break and treat them to a
delicious picnic.

* * * * * * * * * * * *

* * * * * * * * * * * *

Keep abreast of when
meteor showers and
shooting stars are likely
to appear where you are,
and enjoy the *spectacle*.

* * * * * * * * * * * *

* * * * * * * * * * *

Take a *holiday* to a
northern country and see
the *aurora borealis*
(the Northern Lights).

* * * * * * * * * * *

GOOD THINGS COME TO THOSE WHO WAIT.

★ ★ ★ ★ ★ ★ ★ ★ ★ ★ ★ ★

Find a subject you're
passionate about and
take a course – or even
a degree – in it.

★ ★ ★ ★ ★ ★ ★ ★ ★ ★ ★ ★

* * * * * * * * * * * *

Take a *journey* on
one of the world's great
scenic railways, such as
the West Highland Line
in Scotland.

* * * * * * * * * * * *

★ ★ ★ ★ ★ ★ ★ ★ ★ ★ ★ ★ ★

Host a *family reunion*
and invite your entire
extended family.

★ ★ ★ ★ ★ ★ ★ ★ ★ ★ ★ ★ ★

★ ★ ★ ★ ★ ★ ★ ★ ★ ★ ★ ★

YEARS WRINKLE THE SKIN, BUT TO GIVE UP ENTHUSIASM WRINKLES THE SOUL.

SAMUEL ULLMAN

★ ★ ★ ★ ★ ★ ★ ★ ★ ★ ★ ★

* * * * * * * * * * * *

Write a *letter to yourself*
at 70 and put it somewhere
safe for you to find in a
decade's time.

* * * * * * * * * * * *

* * * * * * * * * * *

Read *The Prophet*
by Kahlil Gibran, and
explore other philosophical
literature. Encourage
others to read it and use it
to start a discussion on
the human condition.

* * * * * * * * * * *

* * * * * * * * * * * * *

Get a *metal detector*
and comb your local
beach or common for
buried treasure.

* * * * * * * * * * * * *

* * * * * * * * * * * *

Dedicate a day
to yourself: make your
favourite breakfast, have a
long luxurious bath, book
yourself a massage and do
everything you enjoy.

* * * * * * * * * * * *

* * * * * * * * * * * * *

Learn to make your favourite *takeaway dish.* It'll be cheaper, and you may even be able to *improve* upon it!

* * * * * * * * * * * * *

ALL'S WELL THAT ENDS WELL.

* * * * * * * * * * * *

Attend or host a
murder mystery
evening, and let your
inner *sleuth* take over.

* * * * * * * * * * * *

* * * * * * * * * * * *

Take up *wild swimming*
in the sea — float on your
back in the *buoyant*
saltiness and feel
invigorated.

* * * * * * * * * * * *

* * * * * * * * * * * * *

Make a warming
winter soup to share
with friends and family
on a *cold day*.

* * * * * * * * * * * * *

TIME AND TIDE WAIT FOR NO MAN.

★ ★ ★ ★ ★ ★ ★ ★ ★ ★ ★ ★

Learn *mirror writing,* in the style of *Leonardo da Vinci.*

★ ★ ★ ★ ★ ★ ★ ★ ★ ★ ★ ★

★ ★ ★ ★ ★ ★ ★ ★ ★ ★ ★ ★

Grow your own food!
Fruit, veg or herbs can all be
grown in your garden or in
a *window box.*

★ ★ ★ ★ ★ ★ ★ ★ ★ ★ ★ ★

* * * * * * * * * * * *

Go to a *haunted house*
or dungeon and
scare yourself silly.

* * * * * * * * * * * *

* * * * * * * * * * * *

Give away all the things
in your house you don't need
to people or a *charity*
that could make better
use of them.

* * * * * * * * * * * *

* * * * * * * * * * *

SOME DAY YOU WILL BE OLD ENOUGH TO START READING FAIRY TALES AGAIN.

C. S. LEWIS

* * * * * * * * * * *

If you're interested in finding out more about our gift books, follow us on Twitter:
@Summersdale

www.summersdale.com